Frog in a Well

Turning obstacles to opportunities

By Harold D'Souza

Frog in a Well: Turning obstacles to opportunities

Printed in the United States © Copyright 2019, by Harold D'Souza

ISBN: 9781687015402

Published by Harold D'Souza Press

Address:
9453 Hunters Creek Drive
Cincinnati 45242-6661

Email: hrdsouza17@gmail.com

Phone: 513-620-9589

Publishing Consultant
Bukola Oriola Group, LLC
info@bukolaoriola.com

The Prologue

Labor trafficking and debt bondage in the United States of America is just the "Tip of the Iceberg".

We never had running water and electricity growing up in India. The concept of restroom and bathroom never prevailed in those days. Every family will draw water from the "Well". In every well, there is a frog. The frog believes, this is his world, not knowing there is a better world outside of the "Well". Similarly, a victim in human trafficking believes that living under the control of the "Perpetrator" is the only "World". The victim is manipulated, tricked and trapped by the "Perpetrator". The victim is mesmerized by the trafficker, unable to understand that there is a better world with happiness, respect, choice, care and freedom.

My goal is to cultivate hope, courage, resilience and freedom for all. Suicide or silence is neither a solution, nor an option or choice. Every situation in life should be overcome in an optimistic style, even if you are in a vulnerable position, be it critical health, financial crisis, unemployment, broken relationship, child abuse, or victim of labor and/or sex trafficking.

Never quit, accept and own your problems, victory will be yours forever. Stigma, shame, sorrow, and struggles are the path to success. Live your life to the fullest. Three things to take away from my journey of slavery to success are; be happy, be empowered and be thankful.

God Bless America!

Your friend,
Harold D'Souza

Survivors are poor starters, but strong finishers.

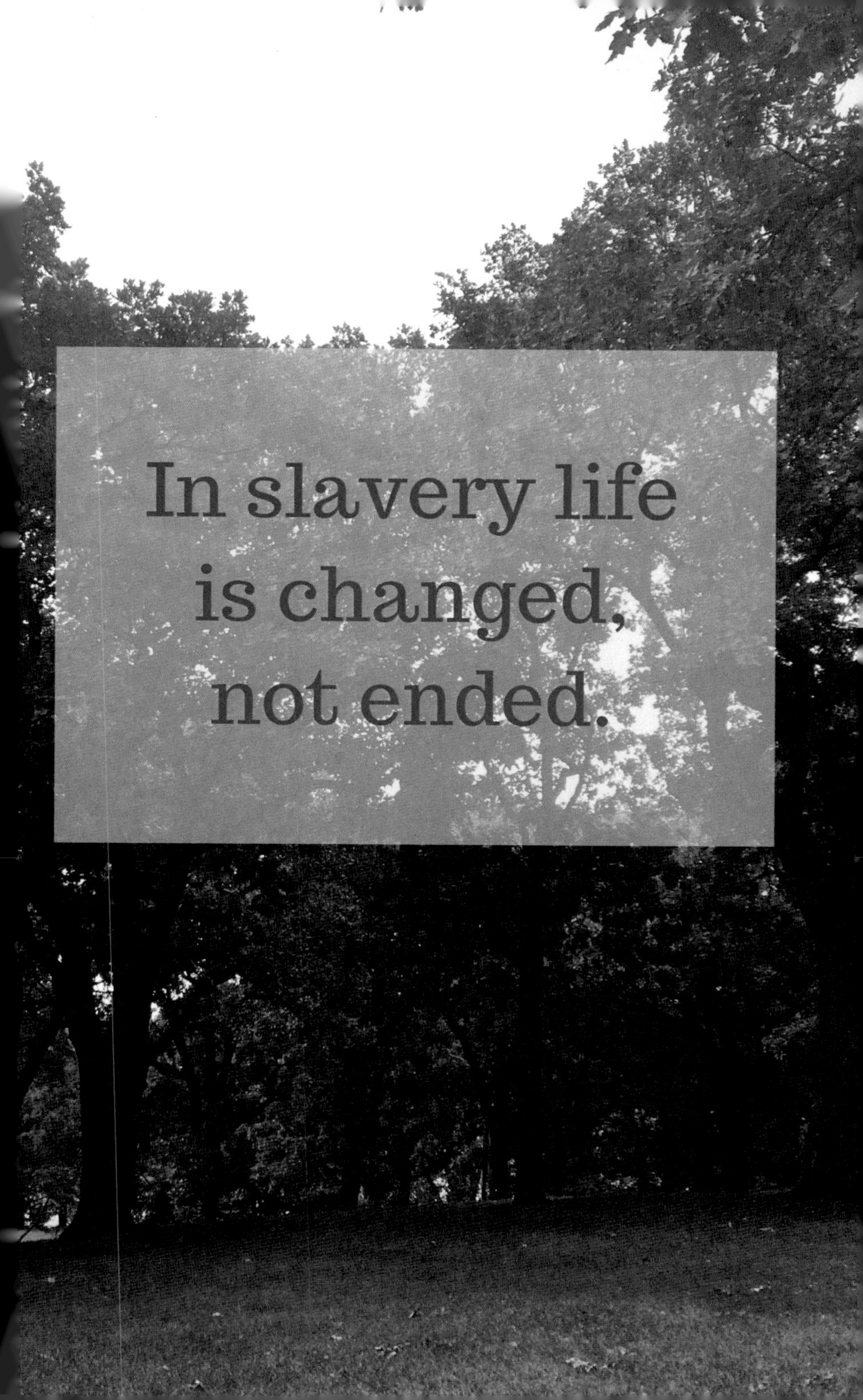
In slavery life
is changed,
not ended.

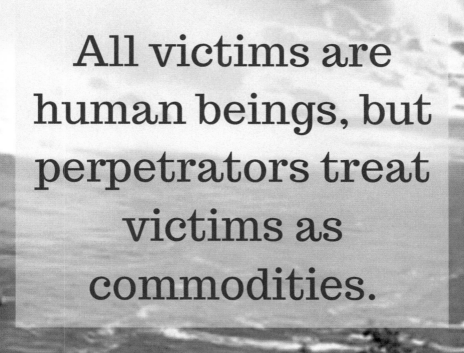

All victims are human beings, but perpetrators treat victims as commodities.

Making a mistake is not a mistake,
Making no mistake is a mistake,
Repeating a mistake is a big mistake,
Learning from your mistake to empower other victims to live a happy life is not a mistake.

In survivors life healing does not mean the trauma never existed. It means the trauma no longer controls our life.

There is no expiration date for a trauma in a survivor's life. Even if the trauma occurred 20 years ago.

Do not be scared what the child speaks, but be scared what the child sees or hears.

In a victims life the time never ticks. Every second is like a minute. Every minute is like an hour. Every hour is like a day. Every day is like a month and Every month is like a year.

When a perpetrator "SLAPS" your child in front of your eyes; The child is hurt for 60 seconds but the father's heart is hurt for life.

Desire changes nothing,
Decision changes something,
Determination changes everything.

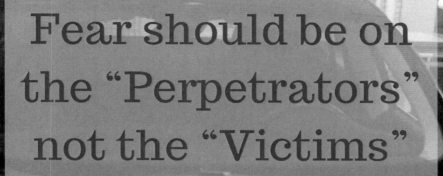

Fear should be on
the "Perpetrators"
not the "Victims"

END HUMAN TRAFFICKING

FREEDOM5000.ORG

#RECORDFORFREEDOM

The best and most beautiful moments in the life of a "Survivor" is to experience their kids prosper with freedom.

Survivors do not have the time, money or resources but they have the heart, passion and purpose to uplift victims.

People should respect you not your chair.

When you do charity with your right hand your left hand should not know.

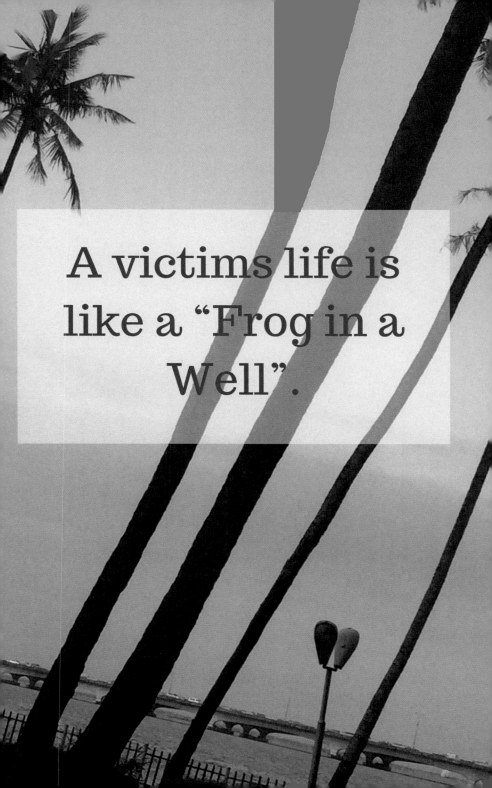

A victims life is like a "Frog in a Well".

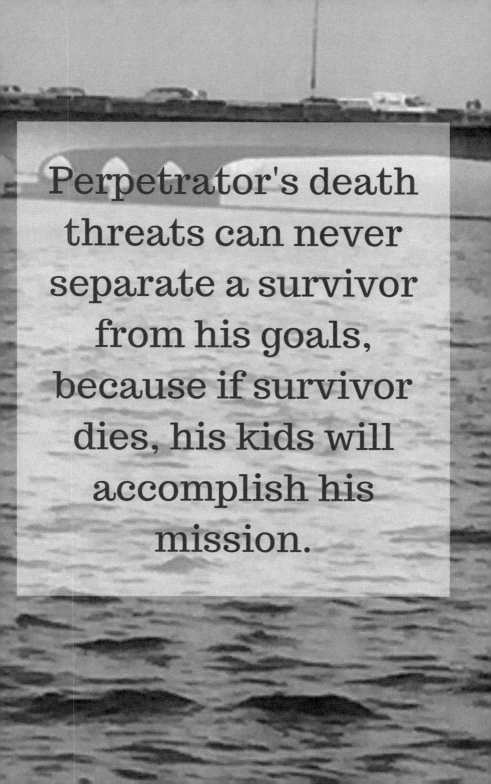

Perpetrator's death threats can never separate a survivor from his goals, because if survivor dies, his kids will accomplish his mission.

Never
underestimate the
power of a survivor.

Every survivor has his or her own beauty, but not everyone can see it.

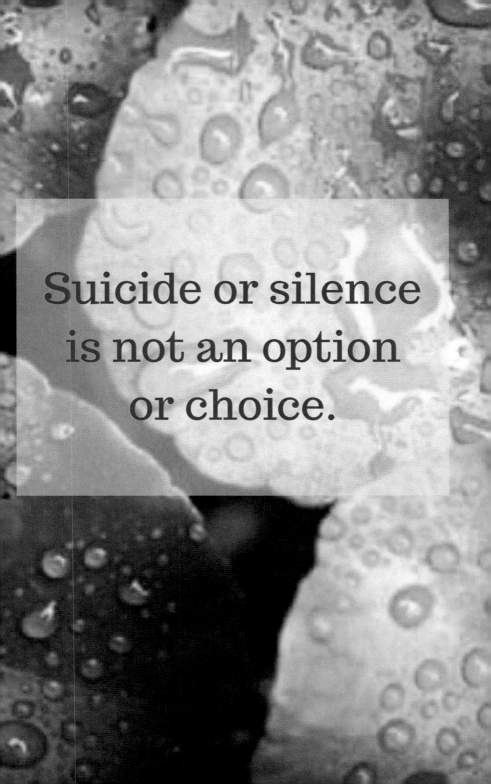

Suicide or silence
is not an option
or choice.

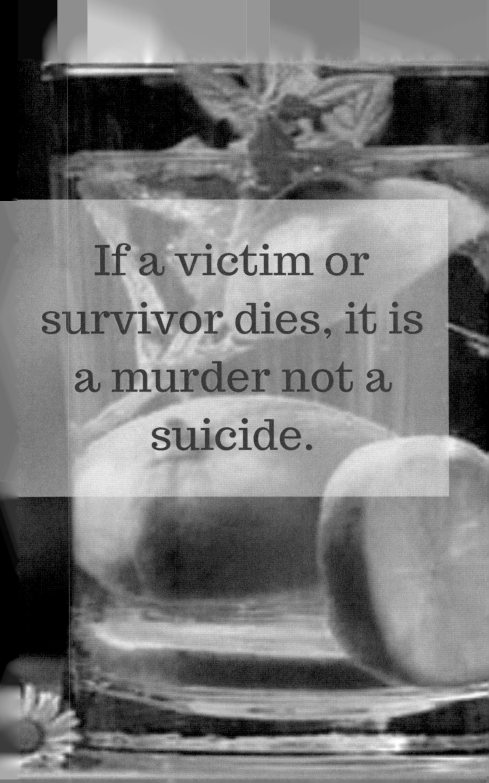

If a victim or survivor dies, it is a murder not a suicide.

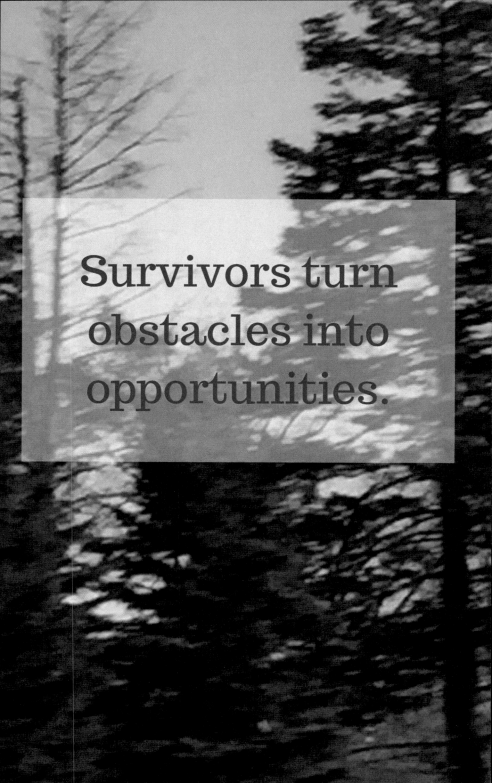

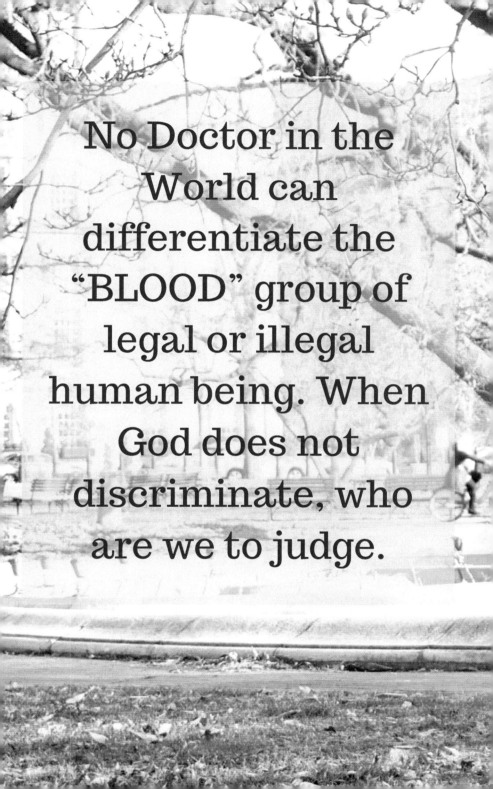

No Doctor in the World can differentiate the "BLOOD" group of legal or illegal human being. When God does not discriminate, who are we to judge.

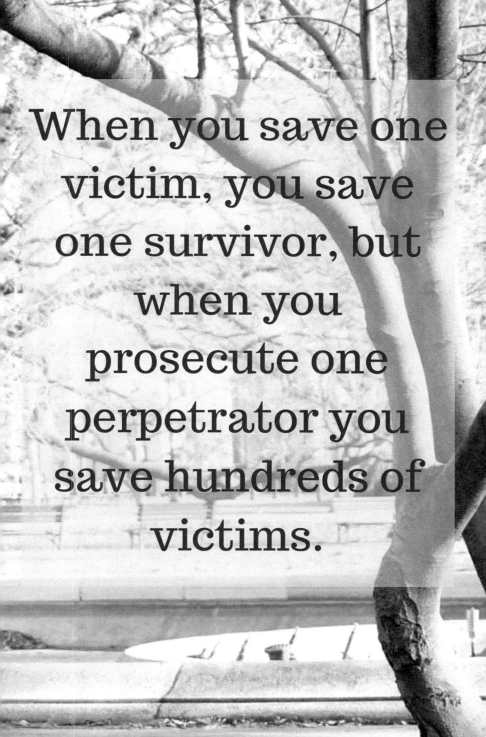

When you save one victim, you save one survivor, but when you prosecute one perpetrator you save hundreds of victims.

Struggle is a path to success. Failure is a path to freedom. Hurt is a path to happiness. Stigma is a path to strength. Never Quit! Suicide or silence is not a solution.

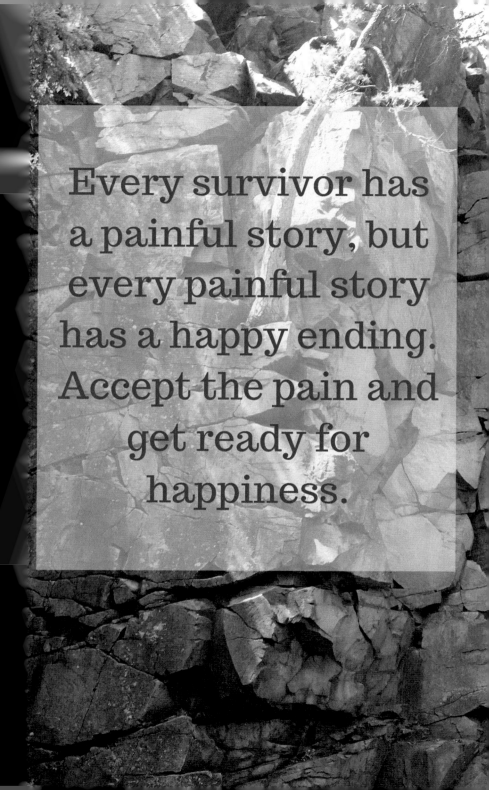

Every survivor has a painful story, but every painful story has a happy ending. Accept the pain and get ready for happiness.

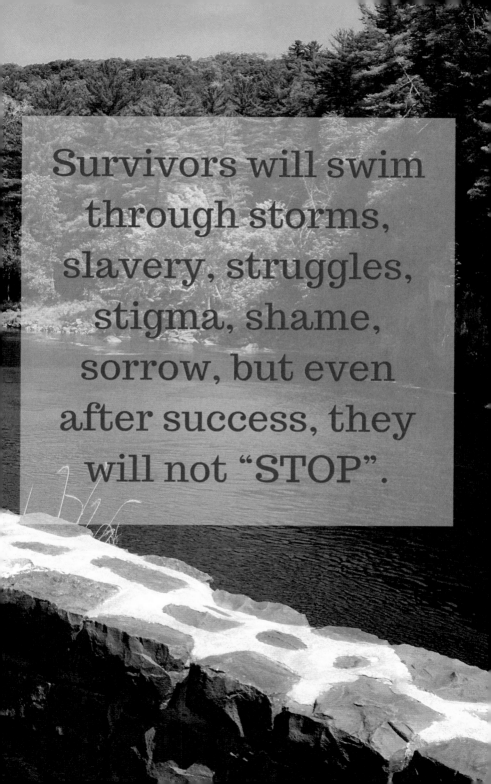

Survivors will swim through storms, slavery, struggles, stigma, shame, sorrow, but even after success, they will not "STOP".

Look, listen, learn, laugh and love with every survivor.

Strength does not come from winning, but when a survivor decides not to surrender that is strength.

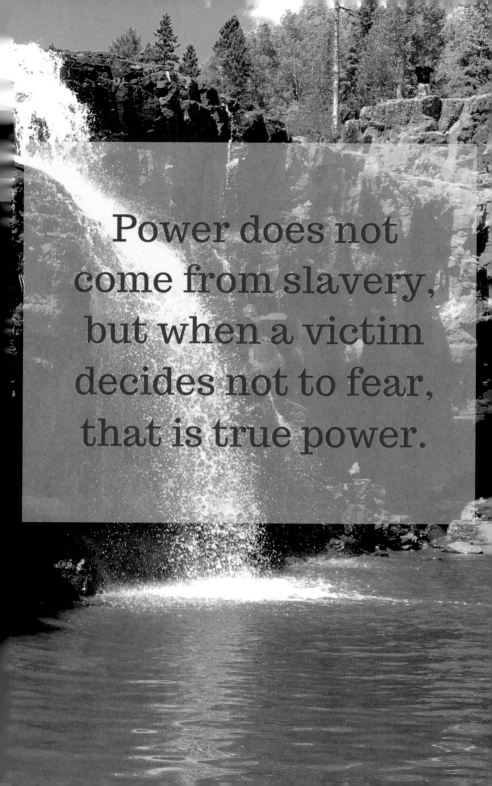

Power does not come from slavery, but when a victim decides not to fear, that is true power.

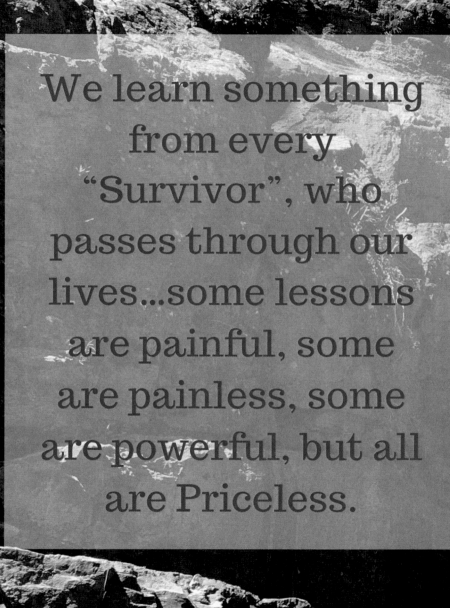

We learn something from every "Survivor", who passes through our lives...some lessons are painful, some are painless, some are powerful, but all are Priceless.

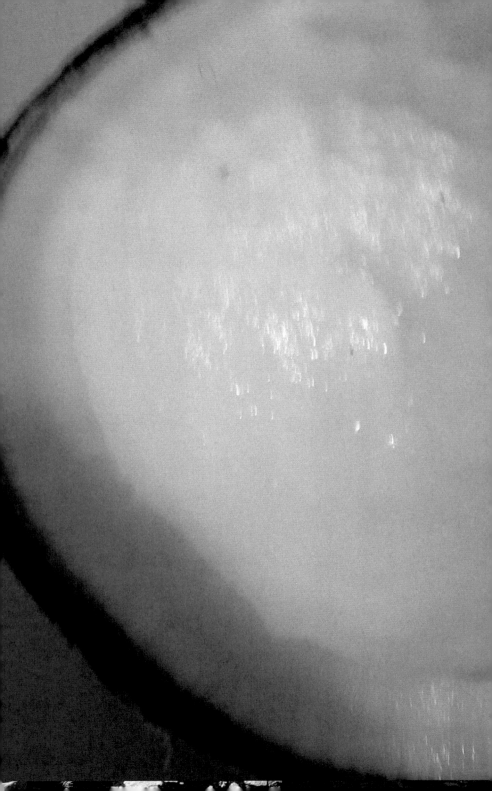

Survivors sharpen society, and survivors will save the society from slavery.

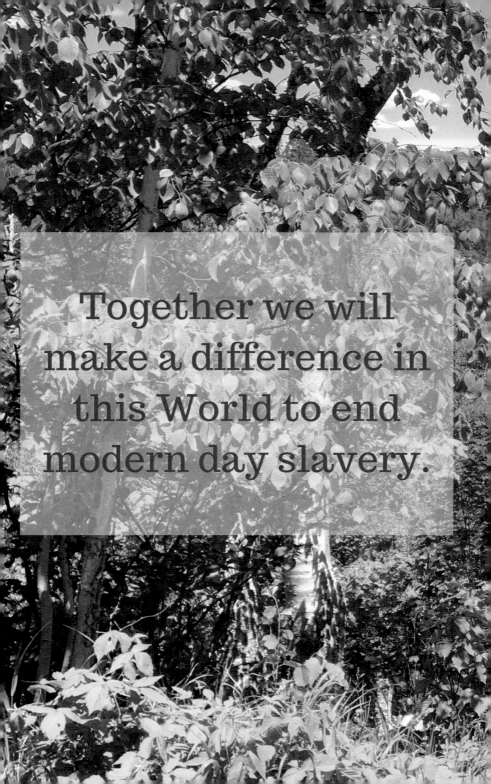

Together we will make a difference in this World to end modern day slavery.

When your faith is deep, there is no reason to fear the perpetrators.

Men:
Focus on companionship not marriage, Focus on delighting not satisfying, Focus on caring, not controlling, Focus on ours, not mine, Focus on Wife not Life. Happiness is forever.

The height of candles may differ, but they yield the same brightness. It is not the perpetrators, but the survivors who shine in the society.

Survivors' failure and success should not be measured by their fall, but by how fast survivors pick themselves up.

When Snake and Mongoose fight, mongoose always win. Similarly, in perpetrators' and survivors' battle, survivors win.
Law of nature. Honesty prevails. Victim-Survivors......Rise-Fight-Victory is yours.

After freedom, the air I breathe, the food I eat, the water I drink, all tastes different.

Never abuse a child, because after few years, he will be the prosecutor for the same perpetrator.

If your eyes are positive, you will love the victims. If your tongue is positive, the victims will love you, but   If your heart is positive the world will love you.

Do not tell GOD how big the STORM is in you life, but tell the STORM how big GOD is in your life.